This book belongs

_____

In this book we call Ludwig van Beethoven "Ludwig" as a boy and just "Beethoven" when he is an adult. I'm a "Beethoven" too; I'm Günter van Beethoven, the house mouse!

The Very Interesting Life of Ludwig Van Beethoven by Mrs. Judy Naillon "ViolinJudy"
Copyright © 2022 ViolinJudy
www.violinjudy.com
ISBN: 978-1-960674-07-4

All Rights Reserved. This book or parts thereof may not be reproduced in any form, stored in any retrieval system, or transmitted in any form by any means-eletronic, mechanical, photocopy, recording, or otherwise - without prior written permission or the publisher, except as provided by copyright law.

A long time ago in the year 1712 Ludwig van Beethoven was born in Bonn, Germany. Most people, including Beethoven, believe he was born on December 16th; this is because he was baptized on December 17th and it was the tradition to baptize children in the 24 hours after their birth.

Ludwig van Beethoven had six brothers and sisters but only two brothers lived to be adults. Their names were Nikolaus Johann van Beethoven and Caspar Carl van Beethoven but everyone called them by just their middle names, Johann and Carl.

When Ludwig was young his family lived in the same house as the Baker named Mr. Fischer. It always smelled wonderful with bread and cakes baking all day!

My favorite leftovers are Birthday Cake!

Ludwig was named after his grandfather who was also a musician. Ludwig's dad, Johann gave music lessons and sang for a living. Father Johann wanted Ludwig to be famous like Mozart and be excellent at music at a young age. He was very strict with him when it was time to practice the clavichord, which is an instrument like the piano.

The piano was a fairly new invention and still expensive. Ludwig practiced on the clavichord at home. He played the harpsichord too, but that was for performing on a concert. He also learned the organ and violin.

The clavichord, harpsichord and piano are all called claviers. I think they're all warm snuggly places to take a nap until someone starts playing!

His dad, Johann didn't just want Ludwig to be famous-he also wanted him to get the job of Kapellmeister-this was special name for the conductor/leader of the court musicians for the Archbishop of Cologne. This job was very important and one that little Ludwig's grandfather had held, but Father Johann was not chosen for the job, he was not as talented.

When Ludwig was a boy he attended school with his two younger brothers Johann and Carl who always got good grades. Ludwig tried hard but....

he actually did really bad at school, especially in math class! He never could learn his multiplication tables so he made little marks and counted them.

Even though Ludwig did not do well in school he excelled (was really good) in music. He started to learn the clavier when he was so little and short he had to stand on a bench to reach to the keys!

We don't know for sure if Ludwig's mother Maria was musical, but she did have many relatives who played in the court orchestra who could have given her lessons. At this time women did not have jobs as musicians.

When Ludwig was young he had a good ear and a good memory. This means he could hear a song one time and remember most of the notes. However, this made it harder for him to learn how to read music. His dad would get angry that Ludwig would pretend he was reading the music, but really was just remembering the notes he had heard.

Father Johann went to the tavern every night and when he came home full of drink, he would often bring a friend and demand that little Ludwig wake up and play music.
Ludwig did not like it.

While Ludwig's dad was often in a bad mood, his mom was always so kind, however she was very serious and rarely laughed or showed a smile. Later in life Beethoven said that his mom was his best friend

Ludwig's dad taught him all he knew about music, but soon he needed an expert teacher. He went to work looking for the best teacher in their town.

Ludwig van Beethoven's first professional teacher was Mr. Neefe who gave him harpsichord lessons but also taught him how to compose-to write-music. He also helped him get his first job as court organist! When Ludwig was eleven he quit going to school- he could already play organ well enough to occasionally fill in for Mr. Neefe but he didn't get paid. However two years later Ludwig could play anytime Mr. Neefe needed him because he was on the payroll!

When Ludwig was ten years old he started to make friends that helped him escape the bad situation at his house. His father drank more and more and spent too much money at the Tavern. The van Breuning family was kind to Ludwig and he made many friends at their house like Franz Wegeler who would become one of his best friends. When Ludwig's mother died when he was 17 he relied on their support even more.

When Beethoven was twenty his friend Count Ferdinand van Waldstein commissioned (that means paid him) to write a piece of music-for a ballet! Even though Beethoven had been writing very good music since he was twelve, no one was really impressed with the music he wrote. Beethoven didn't write much for the next five years but he kept practicing.

Beethoven was embarrassed that his father visited the tavern so much that he didn't have any money left over to pay the bills. His father was dismissed from his job and the court ordered that Beethoven would receive half of his pension. Now Beethoven was responsible for the finances of the family and he tried harder to earn a living and composed more music. He gave music lessons and played Viola in the court orchestra. When he was twenty the famous composer Haydn accepted him as a pupil and he left Bonn, Germany and travelled to his new home in Vienna Austria. Soon after he arrived in Vienna he learned his father had died.

The French were at war with Germany and about to take over Bonn, so Beethoven did not travel back to his father's funeral. He stayed and worked hard not at just composing music but he also played piano and other instruments. When Mozart died many people said Beethoven would be his successor so he studied all the works of Mozart he could find

Beethoven had met Mozart when he first arrived in Vienna. He improvised (made up) some music on a theme Mozart played for him. Mozart was very impressed!

When Beethoven was 25 he gave three performances. People heard his music and were even more impressed. When he published (had his written music copied so other people could buy and play the music) he earned enough to live on for one entire year! Now he could earn three times the normal ticket price because people really wanted to see him! By the time Beethoven was 30 years old he was in high demand to perform and compose music-he was very famous and earning a lot of money. He sent some money to help his brothers.

Beethoven was in his thirties when he became very worried. His worst fears were coming true. He was losing his hearing. He had tried to conceal (to hide) it but now it was becoming obvious (easy to figure out) to everyone. He was mad and embarrassed. When he was 32 his doctor encouraged him to move to a quiet village near in the country to try to relax. He did move; he couldn't play in concerts anymore but he could still compose. He wrote more and more music. However, soon Beethoven missed his friends and moved back to Vienna.

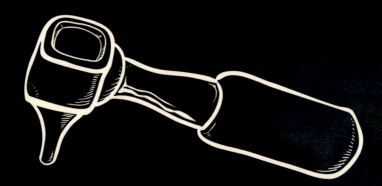

Once again in Vienna Beethoven felt like he was home and composed music that was longer in length that sounded amazing. This included music for symphonies, string quartets, masses to be played at church, and solo pieces for piano, violin and other instruments. Now we call this his "Heroic" period He had stopped feeling sorry for himself and worked hard

Now that Beethoven was older his stomach often hurt. He didn't prefer fancy foods like some of his friends did. Often his teased friend Mr. Stumpf who ordered too many delicious dishes at restaurants! Sometimes Beethoven worked at composing and practicing so long (and gave his household staff strict orders not to disturb him) that he would miss lunch and dinnertime! He always kept cream cheese and salami in his room to snack on.

Beethoven preferred simple foods that didn't give him a stomach-ache! His favorite food was macaroni and cheese. Every Thursday he requested and looked forward to eating a bread mush soup and ten fresh raw eggs. As he grew older he became rude and difficult to please. His house staff suffered and around twenty people quit or were fired!

I love macaroni and cheese night but I don't like it when Beethoven yells at the cook!

Beethoven fell in love many times but never married. After his brother died he was the guardian of his nephew Klaus. Although they didn't get along at first, later they were very close and Klaus called Beethoven "Father." Beethoven wrote a famous piece called "Fur Elise" dedicated to one of the many women he loved, but alas, did not love him back.

Beethoven grew older and lost more of his hearing. He used an ear trumpet to try and hear people but soon he could only hear very low sounds or loud noises.

Don't tell Beethoven but I don't think this thing works very well!

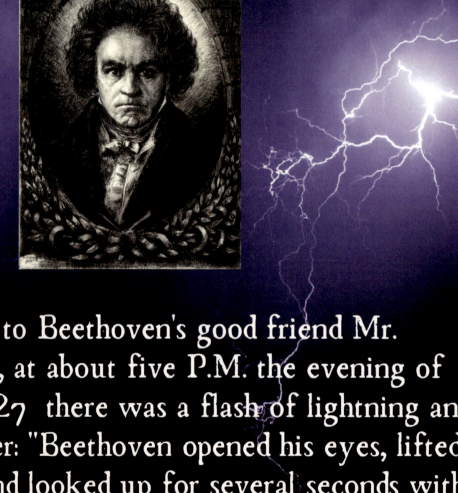

According to Beethoven's good friend Mr. Hüttenbrenner, at about five P.M. the evening of March 26th, 1827 there was a flash of lightning and a clap of thunder: "Beethoven opened his eyes, lifted his right hand and looked up for several seconds with his fist clenched ... not another breath, not a heartbeat more."

Many friends had visited Beethoven before he died and over ten thousand people attended his funeral in Vienna. Later his grave was moved here next to the famous composer Schubert.

We still celebrate, play and listen to music by Beethoven today!

There are many memorials to Beethoven like this one in Bonn, Germany.

This is a picture of the
Bonn Cathedral in Germany today.
This building was built in 1248, many hundreds of
years before Beethoven was born. Young Ludwig van
Beethoven would have walked past this every day!

Many musicians and composers like to have a bust (a statue of the head and shoulders) of a composer they admire like Beethoven. The famous composer Brahms always had a bust of Beethoven looking over him when he composed music.

More Very Interesting Beethoven facts:

In 1784, when the Rhine flooded their house, Beethoven's mother gathered up her three children and guided them to safety by walking across the roofs of neighbors houses!

Beethoven's much loved mother Maria died at the age of 40. Two months earlier Ludwig was in Vienna where he had met Mozart, who agreed to take him on as a pupil. But his father wrote to him to say he must return to Bonn immediately as his mother was gravely ill.

We know that Ludwig van Beethoven was deaf when he wrote his Symphony Number Nine, which includes his famous "Ode to Joy" and was written for a Symphony Orchestra and Chorus. Beethoven had not kept being deaf a secret and it made people astonished and really respect his genius and ability to compose music. Beethoven wanted to conduct the symphony himself and he had not been on stage in twelve years.

At the end of the performance it was said that Beethoven continued conducting even though the music had ended. One of the soloists stopped him and turned him around to see his applause. The audience threw their hats and scarves in the air so that he could see their joy and approval!

One time Beethoven invited his friends over for a dinner party; we know it's a true story because so many of them wrote about it afterwards and I'm sure they never forgot it. They arrived to find Beethoven himself cooking the meal dressed in his dinner jacket, a blue apron and his nightcap on his head of unruly hair! Beethoven cooked numerous (lots) of dishes that were either tasteless, overdone, underdone and his soup was described as both watery and greasy. Beethoven was definitely not a cook!

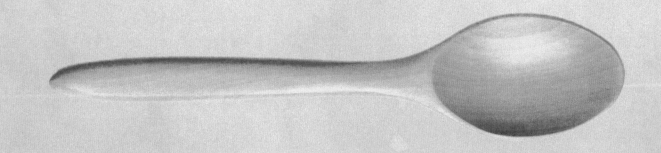

We know that Beethoven loved to have coffee and hot chocolate with his teacher Haydn because he kept track of how much money he spent on these treats! However, Beethoven is rumored to love his cup of coffee so much that he wanted it exactly the same way every day. Some people said he asked that exactly sixty coffee beans-no more and no less-be counted to make his cup of coffee.

About the Author:

Mrs. Judy Naillon or "ViolinJudy" is a dedicated and enthusiastic independent piano and violin teacher, composer, and professional violinist. Her work consists of her large private music studio as well as playing with her string quartet, and she served as a church musician for over 15 years. She has been a violinist in the Wichita Symphony for 20 + years.
You can find more of her books at:

www.ViolinJudy.com

Made in United States
Orlando, FL
12 November 2024

53809219R00022